ADOBE LIGHTROOM 2025

GUIDEBOOK

Mastering Modern Photo Editing

from Desktop to Mobile

John Michael

Table of Contents

Learning Resources, Communities, and Updates145

Chapter One

Introduction

What Is Adobe Lightroom?

I still remember the first time I opened Adobe Lightroom. I was juggling dozens of client projects—brand shoots, editorial layouts, social media campaigns—and my workflow was in chaos. I had raw files scattered across hard drives and edits lost in folders labeled "final_final2.psd." Lightroom changed everything.

At its core, **Adobe Lightroom is a powerful photo editing and organizing tool**, designed specifically for photographers and visual creatives who need both precision and speed. It's not just another editing app—it's a visual command center. Unlike Photoshop, which offers pixel-level editing, Lightroom is non-destructive. That means your original image is never touched. Every change you make—from exposure tweaks to cinematic color grading—is layered as metadata. You can always roll back, rework, or repurpose without losing a thing.

What I love most is how Lightroom mirrors the creative flow. You're not bogged down by cluttered menus or buried tools. Whether you're color-correcting an entire wedding shoot or fine-tuning the lighting in a product shot, Lightroom lets you move fast without compromising quality. It's built for people who work with images every day—and for people who care deeply about how those images make others feel.

For me as a graphic designer, Lightroom isn't just about editing—it's about storytelling. It's the difference between an okay image and one that breathes mood, style, and brand identity.

Overview of the Lightroom Ecosystem (Desktop, Mobile, Cloud)

Adobe didn't stop at building just one version of Lightroom—they built an entire ecosystem around it. And this is where the real magic happens: Lightroom doesn't just live on your desktop anymore. It lives *everywhere* you do.

1. Lightroom Classic (Desktop)

This is the original workhorse. It's the version I rely on when I'm in the studio, editing high-resolution photos on a calibrated monitor.

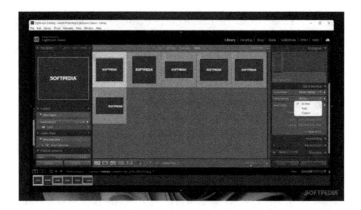

If you're a pro or managing massive libraries, this is where you'll feel at home.Lightroom Classic gives you the most robust toolset: custom keyword tagging, advanced file management, tethered capture, printing options, and batch processing like no other.

2. Lightroom (Cloud-Based Desktop and Web)

Then there's the newer, cloud-based Lightroom—just called "Lightroom." It's sleeker, simplified, and fully integrated with Adobe's Creative Cloud. I use it when I want to sync images across my devices or collaborate remotely.

It's perfect for travel projects or when I need to start edits on my laptop and finish them on my desktop without fussing over drives or folders.

3. Lightroom Mobile (iOS & Android)

Lightroom Mobile has become my pocket studio. Whether I'm on location or just waiting at a café, I can cull images, apply edits, and even export deliverables right from my phone or tablet.

The interface is clean and intuitive, yet powerful enough to handle RAW files and precise adjustments. And thanks to Adobe Sensei's AI tools, I can mask skies or subjects with a single tap. That's huge when you're on a deadline.

4. The Cloud Connection

The unsung hero of the Lightroom ecosystem is the cloud. Adobe's sync functionality means that when

I upload photos from a shoot in Lightroom Mobile, they're instantly available in Lightroom on my desktop. Edits made on one device appear on all others in seconds. It's like your entire library follows you—securely, seamlessly, and without the clutter of hard drives.

Lightroom isn't just an app. It's an interconnected creative environment that adapts to how *you* work. Whether you're editing at your desk, reviewing proofs on your tablet, or color-grading in an airport lounge, Lightroom gives you the tools and the freedom to create without compromise.

What's New in Lightroom 2025

Every year, Adobe seems to push Lightroom further, but 2025 is a landmark update. It's not just about refining the tools—it's about reimagining how we interact with our photos. As someone who edits images daily for design portfolios, brand campaigns, and client presentations, I was genuinely impressed by this year's release. The upgrades aren't gimmicky—they're practical, powerful, and honestly overdue.

1. Real-Time Generative Fill (Powered by Firefly 2)

Yes, the game-changing Photoshop feature has arrived in Lightroom. Now you can *paint in* missing backgrounds, extend compositions, or remove distractions with intelligent generative fill—all without leaving Lightroom.

I tested this on a lifestyle shoot with cluttered city backgrounds. In seconds, the AI filled in skies, blurred signage, and even reconstructed building edges. It saved me hours.

2. Multi-Mask AI Layers

Lightroom 2025 finally allows **multiple AI-powered masks** to coexist on a single image with layer-style logic. You can adjust their stack order, visibility, and blending. I use this to isolate skin tones, enhance product textures, and fine-tune environmental lighting—all non-destructively, and all within one workspace. It feels like Photoshop-level control without the complexity.

3. Color Harmony Panel

Color grading just got smarter. Instead of tweaking color wheels blindly, Lightroom now analyzes your image and suggests **harmonious palettes** using Adobe Sensei's deep color engine. This has been a gift for my design work—no more second-guessing skin tones or mood lighting.

The palettes are beautiful, intentional, and exportable to Illustrator and InDesign for seamless branding work.

4. Preset Studio with AI-Adaptive Variants

Presets are now context-aware. Lightroom analyzes each image's subject, lighting, and mood, then suggests dynamic variations of your presets in real-time. I've built brand-specific preset packs for clients, and with this update, they adapt to each image without flattening style or tone. It's brilliant.

5. Smart Collaboration Tools

Now, I can **invite clients or team members to comment directly on images in the cloud**

library—no more back-and-forth emails or clunky PDFs. Feedback syncs live, making review sessions smoother and faster, especially when I'm working remotely with teams in different time zones.

System Requirements and Installation

Lightroom has always been pretty forgiving when it comes to hardware, but if you want to unlock all of Lightroom 2025's high-performance and AI-based features, you'll need to make sure your setup is up to the task.

Minimum System Requirements (as of 2025)

For Windows

- OS: Windows 11 (22H2 or later)
- Processor: Intel Core i5 (10th Gen or newer) or AMD Ryzen 5
- RAM: 16 GB (32 GB recommended for AI tools)
- GPU: NVIDIA GeForce GTX 1650 or AMD Radeon RX 5500 XT (with 4 GB VRAM minimum)

- Storage: SSD with at least 10 GB free for installation, plus additional space for cache/previews
- Display: 1920x1080 resolution or higher, color-calibrated recommended

For macOS

- OS: macOS 13 Ventura or later
- Processor: Apple Silicon (M1 or M2) or Intel Core i7 (2019 or later)
- RAM: 16 GB (32 GB for professionals handling large RAW workflows)
- GPU: Integrated M1/M2 GPU or dedicated GPU with 4 GB VRAM minimum
- Storage: SSD, 10 GB free for install
- Display: Retina or 4K monitor recommended

Note: AI-based masking and generative features require a GPU that supports DirectX 12 (Windows) or Metal (macOS), and enough RAM for deep learning models to run efficiently.

Installation Tips (Professional Workflow)

From years of experience, here's how I recommend installing and setting up Lightroom 2025 for smooth sailing:

1. **Back Up Your Catalog First** – Always, *always* make a backup of your current Lightroom catalog before upgrading. Adobe usually handles migrations well, but if you work with legacy presets or third-party plugins, protect your archive.

2. **Use the Creative Cloud Desktop App** – Sign in, go to the Apps tab, and click "Update" on Lightroom. Choose between *Lightroom Classic* and *Lightroom (Cloud)* depending on your workflow style.

3. **Clean Install Option** – If you want a fresh start (I do this once a year), uninstall the old version, then reinstall the new one manually. It helps avoid bloat and lingering bugs from previous builds.

4. **Enable GPU Acceleration** – Head to **Edit > Preferences > Performance** and make sure "Use GPU for image processing" is enabled.

It makes a huge difference in brush lag and preview speed.

5. **Sync Your Presets and Profiles** – After installing, re-link your custom presets, color profiles, and LUTs. You'll find this under the "Presets" tab. I also sync my export presets for branding consistency across client projects.

Chapter Two

Getting Started

Navigating the Lightroom Interface

When you first open Lightroom, it might feel a little overwhelming—especially if you're new or coming from Photoshop. But once you learn how it flows, the interface becomes a workspace that's as intuitive as it is powerful. Think of it like a clean, well-organized studio: everything has its place, and every tool is within reach.

Whether you're using **Lightroom Classic** or the **cloud-based Lightroom**, the layout revolves around your creative flow—from organizing your files to editing and exporting.

In Lightroom Classic:

This is the version I use when I'm working on large commercial projects or heavy client batches. The interface is modular, and each module is laid out in a top bar:

- **Library:** Where you import, organize, sort, and tag your images.

- **Develop:** The main editing workspace—where the magic happens.

- **Map, Book, Slideshow, Print, Web:** These are extras, and depending on your workflow, you may rarely use them.

The left panel is for **navigation and presets**, while the right panel handles **adjustments**. In the center is your image view, and beneath it, the filmstrip—a horizontal scroll of your imported photos.

In Lightroom (Cloud Version):

If I'm on the go or working across multiple devices, this is what I use. The interface is more minimal, with a streamlined feel. Instead of modules, you'll see:

- A single panel on the right for **editing tools**, including Light, Color, Effects, Detail, Optics, and Geometry.

- The left side handles **albums and folders**, with your cloud-synced library accessible anywhere.
- At the bottom, you'll see **import options and filters**.

Everything feels lightweight, and edits auto-sync across devices. It's like working in a sketchbook that's always connected to your full design studio.

Pro Tip: I like customizing my panels in Classic. You can right-click on any panel header and toggle visibility. This is great when you want a clean view or a distraction-free editing session.

Importing Your Photos

Before anything else, you've got to get your photos into Lightroom. And this step matters more than most people think. Why? Because your import process sets the tone for everything—how you organize, find, and edit your images later on.

Here's how I approach importing, whether it's a brand shoot or a folder of travel photos I plan to use for a print layout.

Step-by-Step in Lightroom Classic:

1. **Click the Import Button (Bottom Left, Library Module)**
   This opens the Import window, which gives you two views: your source (on the left) and destination settings (on the right).

2. **Choose Your Source**
   Lightroom reads from SD cards, cameras, phones, or folders. I usually drag-and-drop from a card reader to ensure speed and avoid camera connection errors.

3. **Select Files**
   You can check or uncheck specific images. I usually do a quick cull right here to avoid importing throwaways.

4. **Choose How to Add Them**
   - **Copy as DNG** – Converts RAW to Adobe's open format (I skip this unless I'm archiving).
   - **Copy** – Most common; makes a copy to your selected folder.
   - **Move** – Moves files from one location to another.

o **Add** – Keeps files in place and just references them (ideal for editing images already on a drive).

5. **Set Your Destination Folder**

   This is key for organization. I use a YYYY-MM-DD format with a project name, like: 2025-04-22_ProductShoot_ClientX.

6. **Apply Presets and Metadata (Optional but Powerful)**

   On import, you can apply a custom preset (for a look), add copyright info, and even keyword your photos. This saves hours later when you're filtering or exporting.

7. **Click Import and Let It Work**

In Lightroom (Cloud):

- Just click the **"+" icon** and choose "Add Photos."
- Files will upload directly into your cloud library.
- You can organize them into **Albums** immediately or drag them later.

Everything auto-syncs, and there's less friction—but also fewer options for metadata and structure, which is why I stick to Classic for most professional jobs.

Importing isn't glamorous, but it's the foundation of everything you'll do in Lightroom. A little time spent organizing now means you won't be hunting for missing files or struggling to remember which version was final. I've learned this the hard way—especially when deadlines are tight.

The interface may differ slightly depending on which Lightroom version you're using, but the end goal is the same: get your photos in, keep them organized, and start creating with confidence.

Organizing with Catalogs and Albums

Organization in Lightroom isn't just about keeping your files tidy—it's about building a system that saves you time, supports your workflow, and helps you stay creative instead of constantly hunting for files. Whether you're managing client shoots, personal passion projects, or thousands of assets for design mockups, the way you organize your work in Lightroom determines how efficiently you can get in, make your edits, and get out.

Catalogs in Lightroom Classic

In **Lightroom Classic**, everything revolves around the **catalog**. Think of a catalog as a digital filing cabinet—it stores information *about* your photos, not the images themselves. That means your RAW files still live wherever you store them (external drive, local disk, etc.), and Lightroom just keeps track of them.

As a working designer, I keep separate catalogs for major areas of my work:

- **Client Work** – for paid commercial shoots and branding projects.
- **Personal Projects** – for photo essays, editorial layouts, and my passion for travel photography.
- **Stock and Archive** – for licensed content and older jobs I still reference for inspiration.

Tip: You don't need a separate catalog for every shoot. Keep one catalog per *category* of work. Opening and switching catalogs takes time—avoid making your workflow slower than it needs to be.

Catalogs also store your edits, metadata, and even virtual copies of images. Nothing is destructive here—every tweak you make is stored as a set of instructions, not baked into the image until you export.

Albums and Folders in Lightroom (Cloud)

In the **cloud-based Lightroom**, the structure shifts a little. Here, you're using **Albums**, which act more like smart collections or visual folders. The big difference? All your images are stored in the Adobe Cloud, so you're working across devices seamlessly.

I use Albums to stay organized by:

- Project name or client
- Photo type (portraits, products, locations)
- Phase of work (raw selects, edited finals, exports)

You can also **tag photos with keywords** and use **star ratings** or **flags** to mark your best shots, which helps during the review and export process.

Albums in Lightroom aren't tied to physical storage, which makes them ideal for mobile-first workflows and quick sharing with clients.

Understanding File Formats and Image Resolution

As a graphic designer, this part is crucial. Understanding file formats and resolution isn't just about making your images look good—it's about making sure they're usable, printable, and responsive to whatever project they're meant for.

Whether I'm exporting for a 10-foot print or a web hero banner, choosing the right format and resolution affects everything.

Common File Formats in Lightroom

- **RAW** – The holy grail of image data. These are unprocessed files straight from your camera. Every pixel is preserved, and that gives you full editing freedom. Lightroom handles RAW beautifully, and if you're serious about color grading, this is where you want to start.

- **JPEG** – Compressed and baked-in. Great for web delivery or quick sharing, but every save degrades quality slightly. I use JPEGs for client previews, mood boards, and casual use—but never for final exports that go to press.

- **TIFF** – Lossless and high-quality, ideal for print. If I'm designing a poster, billboard, or magazine spread, I export my final images from Lightroom as TIFFs. They retain layers (if coming from Photoshop) and offer precise color fidelity.

- **DNG (Digital Negative)** – Adobe's open-standard RAW format. Some cameras shoot directly in DNG, but Lightroom can also convert RAWs to DNG during import. I use this for long-term archives—it's compact but still editable.
- **PSD** – Not natively exported from Lightroom, but if you're hopping into Photoshop, Lightroom lets you send images as PSDs for layered editing.

Image Resolution Explained

Resolution is simply **how much detail your image holds**, usually measured in **PPI (pixels per inch)** for print and **pixel dimensions** for screen.

Here's how I break it down in real projects:

- **Web/Screen Use:**
  - Resolution: 72 PPI
  - Format: JPEG or PNG
  - Size: Depends on where it's going (e.g., 1920×1080 for full-screen hero images)

- **Social Media:**
  - Instagram prefers 1080px wide images. Use JPEGs at high quality.
  - Facebook and Twitter compress heavily, so sharpen slightly before export.
- **Print:**
  - Resolution: 300 PPI minimum
  - Format: TIFF or high-quality JPEG
  - Size: Match your document layout in inches and multiply by 300 for pixel count.

Example: An 8"x10" print at 300 PPI = 2400 × 3000 pixels.

Knowing your way around catalogs and albums is what keeps your Lightroom world manageable. And understanding file formats and resolution? That's what keeps your images looking sharp and professional wherever they go—whether on a billboard, a client website, or a social feed.

In my work, these aren't just technical steps—they're part of the craft. They help me protect quality, move quickly, and deliver confidently, knowing every image is print-ready or web-optimized the moment it leaves my screen.

Chapter Three

Library Module

When I'm working with hundreds—or sometimes thousands—of images from a shoot, the **Library Module** is where my organization begins. This is Lightroom Classic's digital contact sheet. It's fast, efficient, and built to help you sort, tag, and prep your images before they ever touch the Develop panel.

This module isn't just about browsing. It's about filtering the noise, finding the gems, and laying the groundwork for a smooth editing session.

Using the Grid and Loupe Views

These are your two primary ways of viewing images inside the Library Module.

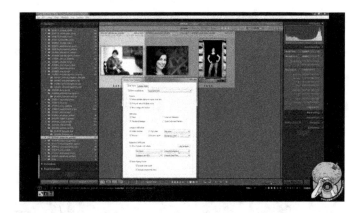

Grid View (G key)

This is your high-level view. Think of it like laying out a whole roll of film on a light table. You can see dozens of images at once, quickly scan compositions, compare exposures, and start organizing.

I use Grid View to:

- Flag the best shots quickly
- Apply ratings in bulk
- Drag images into collections or folders

- Run metadata or keywording across a full set

You can adjust thumbnail size with the slider at the bottom right to zoom in or out on your layout.

Loupe View (E key)

When you want to focus on a single image without editing it yet, this is where you go. It's great for double-checking focus or evaluating expressions during a portrait shoot.

I often toggle between Loupe and Compare (C key) when narrowing down client selects—especially for product work or editorial portraits where nuance matters.

Pro Tip: Hit **Tab** to hide both side panels for a clean, distraction-free review session.

Rating, Flagging, and Labeling Photos

As a working designer, one of the most powerful parts of my Lightroom workflow is my **culling system**. After a shoot, I don't waste time—every image either gets marked or ignored. Over time, this turns into muscle memory.

Here's the system I use:

Flags

- **P (Pick)** – This is a "yes." If I see potential, it gets flagged.
- **X (Reject)** – This is a hard "no." Out of focus, bad expression, blown highlights—it goes into the reject pile.
- Later, I'll filter out rejected images and delete them or move them to an archive folder.

Star Ratings (1–5 keys)

I use star ratings like phases of a project:

- **1 Star:** Maybe. Worth another look.
- **2 Stars:** Usable. Decent composition or light.
- **3 Stars:** Solid. Good enough for client delivery or design mockups.
- **4 Stars:** Finalists. These get edited.

- **5 Stars:** Portfolio quality. Best of the best.

Color Labels (6–9 keys)

This is where things get personal. You can use color labels however you want. I often customize them per project:

- **Red:** Urgent edit
- **Yellow:** Needs retouching in Photoshop
- **Green:** Ready for export
- **Blue:** Sent to client

You can customize color label meanings in the Metadata > Color Label Set menu.

Creating and Managing Collections

Collections are Lightroom's way of organizing images without duplicating files. I live by collections—they let me stay agile and non-destructive.

Types of Collections

- **Standard Collections:** Manual groups of images. Perfect for client galleries, portfolios, or social media batches.
- **Smart Collections:** Automatically fill based on rules (e.g., "All 5-star images from 2025"). I use these for auto-sorting edited finals or grouping specific camera settings for comparison.
- **Collection Sets:** Folders for grouping multiple collections under one umbrella (e.g., "Brand Campaign 2025" with separate collections for products, portraits, BTS).

To create one, just click the **"+" icon** in the Collections panel and choose your type.

Why Collections Matter

Let's say I've done a full-day brand shoot. I can:

- Build a collection for the client selects
- A separate one for social crops
- Another for final TIFF exports for print

That way, I'm not digging through folders—I just jump straight into the collection I need and get to work.

The Library Module is where the groundwork happens. This is where you separate the "meh" from the magic, build structure into your workflow, and start shaping your creative decisions long before you start adjusting highlights or shadows.

As a designer, this kind of control is everything. I can move fast, stay organized, and know that when I'm in the Develop module, I'm not sorting—I'm creating.

Applying and Managing Keywords

If you've ever spent fifteen minutes scrolling through thousands of images trying to find that one perfect shot from a shoot last spring… you already know why keywords matter. In Lightroom, **keywords are your best friend** when it comes to building a searchable, scalable photo library—especially when your catalog spans years of client work, personal projects, and everything in between.

As a designer, I rely on keywords to quickly locate shots for:

- Reusing assets across campaigns
- Referencing older shoots
- Prepping mood boards
- Matching color schemes or visual tones

How to Apply Keywords

You'll find the **Keywording Panel** on the right side of the Library Module. To apply a keyword:

1. Select one or more photos.
2. Type the keyword into the box.
3. Press Enter—and it's instantly added to your photo's metadata.

You can also use the **Keyword Set** and **Keyword Suggestions** areas to streamline tagging. I keep custom keyword sets for common job types:

- For weddings: bride, groom, ceremony, reception
- For product shoots: bottle, overhead, mockup, label
- For location work: city name, time of day, weather conditions

Tip from experience: Keep keywords simple and lowercase. Use hyphens or underscores only if you absolutely need to (for sorting or web export reasons). Lightroom treats spaces as separators, so "blue sky" becomes two separate tags—"blue" and "sky."

Keyword Hierarchies and Keyword Lists

Lightroom also lets you organize keywords into **hierarchies**. This is a game-changer if you work with lots of thematic content or stock libraries.

For example, I've got a keyword structure like this:

- **People**
  - portraits
  - group shots
  - candid

- **Places**
  - o Amsterdam
  - o NYC
  - o studio

That way, tagging something with "Amsterdam" implicitly links it under "Places," making filtering later even more intuitive.

Use the **Keyword List Panel** to drag, nest, and manage your terms efficiently.

Searching and Filtering with Metadata

Keywords are just the beginning. When you combine them with **metadata filters**, Lightroom turns into a super-powered search engine for your images.

What is Metadata?

Metadata is data *about* your image. Lightroom tracks dozens of fields automatically:

- Camera model
- Lens used

- Exposure settings

- Date and time

- File type

- Aspect ratio

- Keywords and labels

- ISO, shutter speed, aperture

It's all searchable, and that's where the **Filter Bar** at the top of the Library Module comes into play.

Using the Filter Bar

Press the / key or go to **View > Show Filter Bar**. From here, you can filter your images by:

- **Text** – Search by filename, caption, or keyword.

- **Attribute** – Filter by star ratings, color labels, flags.

- **Metadata** – Select specific camera bodies, lenses, dates, or even focal lengths.

Here's a real-world example from my own workflow: Let's say I'm preparing a layout that needs ultra-sharp product shots taken with a 50mm prime. I'll filter:

- Camera: Canon EOS R5
- Lens: 50mm f/1.2
- Rating: 3 stars and above
- Keyword: "product"
  Instantly, I've got exactly what I need—no guesswork, no digging.

Saving Filter Presets

If you run the same search often (like "4-star and up, labeled green"), you can **save that filter as a preset**. This is fantastic for batch workflows or for managing team-based tagging systems across shared catalogs.

This isn't just metadata—it's muscle memory. When you make keywording and filtering a habit, Lightroom stops being just a storage space and becomes a living archive of your creative process. It remembers what you've done, where you've been, and what matters most in your work.

For me, this isn't just about being organized. It's about **trusting my tools** to help me stay in flow, stay inspired, and keep my creative work sharp and accessible—no matter how big my library grows.

Chapter Four

AI-Powered Features in Lightroom 2025

Adobe Lightroom 2025 isn't just a photo editor—it's a smart, context-aware assistant built right into your workflow. As someone who edits dozens of images a day for client campaigns, brand shoots, and print-ready layouts, I've come to rely on Lightroom's AI features for their speed, accuracy, and frankly, their uncanny intuition.

Lightroom 2025 is powered by Adobe Sensei, Adobe's AI engine, and in this version, it feels smarter, faster, and more useful than ever.

AI Masking and Object Selection

AI Masking was already a game-changer when Adobe introduced it, but in 2025, it's been refined to the point where manual selections now feel like a backup plan.

- **Subject Select** now detects complex silhouettes—whether it's a model against a textured backdrop or a product in mixed lighting—and creates cleaner, more accurate masks than ever before.

- **Object Selection** allows me to drag over *any* area—like a watch, a handbag, or even a shadow—and Lightroom intelligently understands the object boundaries and isolates it with precision.

For my design work, this is invaluable. I can boost the clarity on a leather product, dodge the highlight on a metal logo, or apply a soft vignette to a subject in one click—no need to jump to Photoshop.

Tip: You can now save these AI masks as part of your presets, allowing for batch processing with context-aware adjustments.

Generative Fill and Content-Aware Healing

Here's where things get magical.

- **Generative Fill**, now integrated right into Lightroom, lets you extend backgrounds, remove distractions, or fill gaps seamlessly by typing a short prompt or simply dragging a selection box.

I've used it to:

- Extend a canvas for magazine layouts
- Clean up stray elements in location shoots
- Seamlessly replace patchy skies or cluttered sidewalks
- Content-Aware Healing, powered by AI, has become more intelligent with edge detection and texture synthesis. Healing brush strokes now blend flawlessly with the surrounding pixels—even when working with gradients, noise, or mixed textures.

It's subtle, fast, and blends like a dream. The days of cloning over and over are numbered.

AI-Powered Auto Adjustments and Presets

Let's be honest—there was a time when "Auto" was a four-letter word among professionals. But that's changed. In Lightroom 2025, Auto Adjustments feel like a true assistant, trained on professional-grade aesthetics.

When I hit **Auto,** Lightroom now:

- Adjusts exposure based on histogram *and* detected content

- Preserves skin tones while boosting contrast
- Maintains natural color profiles without over-punching saturation

It's the perfect starting point—especially for previewing rough edits or creating proofs for clients quickly.

And when I create custom presets, **AI-Powered Presets** now adapt to each image based on detected subject, lighting, and tone. One preset can subtly adjust itself from image to image. It's not cookie-cutter anymore—it's context-aware editing.

People & Object Recognition for Sorting

This one has saved me **hours** in post.

Lightroom 2025's face and object recognition can now:

- Group people automatically by name or facial similarity
- Tag repeating products or settings (like "white background bottle shot")

- Detect scenes like "outdoor," "studio," or "urban" for smart collections

As a designer, I often revisit old assets for design references or reuse. With smart tagging and object detection, I no longer dig through folders—I just type "model + sunglasses + beach" and Lightroom finds the session instantly.

Adaptive Presets and Style Transfer

Adaptive Presets were one of the biggest "wow" moments in Lightroom 2025 for me. These are presets that **adjust themselves intelligently** based on what's in the photo.

For example:

- A fashion preset might brighten faces and smooth skin without affecting the background.
- A food photography preset will punch contrast and saturation on the plate but leave neutral areas like the table untouched.

Even cooler? **Style Transfer** now lets you borrow the look of one photo—color tone, exposure feel, depth of contrast—and apply it to others with precision. It doesn't just copy settings—it matches the aesthetic **based on image content.**

This has become part of my creative process for moodboards, portfolio consistency, and even for mimicking a client's brand tone across different shoots.

AI in Lightroom 2025 doesn't replace creativity—it frees it. It clears the technical hurdles that used to slow me down, giving me more time to experiment, iterate, and focus on the art direction of each image.

As a designer, these tools don't just make my workflow faster—they make it more thoughtful. I'm editing with intention, speed, and accuracy, without ever sacrificing quality.

Chapter Five

Develop Module: Core Editing Tools

When it comes to photo editing, the **Develop Module** in Lightroom is where the magic happens. This is where I turn raw captures into finished, polished images, whether it's for a client shoot, personal project, or portfolio piece. From exposure tweaks to color grading, the Develop module offers all the essential tools—and some hidden gems—that let me control every aspect of my photo's look.

Working with the Histogram

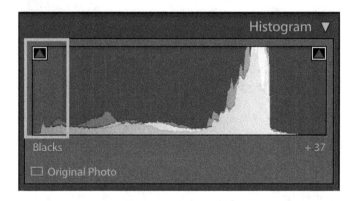

The **Histogram** is one of the most powerful features in Lightroom. It gives you a visual representation of your image's tonal range—from the shadows (on the left) to the highlights (on the right). Here's how I use it:

- **Check for Clipping**: If the histogram's edges are touching the far left or right, you're losing detail in either the shadows or highlights. It's a quick way to spot problems before you make adjustments.

- **Exposure Adjustments**: The histogram helps guide your **Exposure** adjustment. If your histogram is bunched up to the left, your image is underexposed; if it's pushed to the right, you're likely overexposed. Aim for a balanced spread across the middle for a well-exposed photo.

Tip: Click the triangle icons at the top of the histogram to enable **clipping warnings**—they'll highlight areas where you're losing details.

Basic Adjustments: Exposure, Contrast, Highlights, Shadows

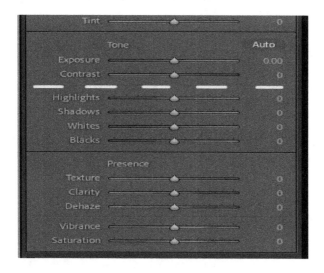

These are your primary controls for adjusting the overall exposure and tone of your image. Let's go through them:

- **Exposure**: Controls the overall lightness or darkness of the image. I use this as my first step in most edits, especially if the image is a bit too dark or too bright.

- **Contrast**: This slider increases or decreases the difference between the light and dark areas of your image. Increasing contrast is great for making a photo feel more dynamic, while lowering contrast can soften the look.

- **Highlights**: This slider specifically targets the brightest parts of your image. Lowering highlights helps recover details in overexposed areas—like skies or reflective surfaces—while boosting highlights can add sparkle to bright areas.

- **Shadows**: Shadows work in the opposite way, brightening or darkening the darker areas of your image. I often use this slider to pull details out of shadowy areas without affecting the rest of the image.

Tip: Use **Alt (Option on Mac)** while adjusting highlights or shadows to see where clipping happens in real-time. It'll turn the clipped areas black or white.

White Balance and Temperature Corrections

White balance is crucial for making your image feel natural or setting a specific mood.

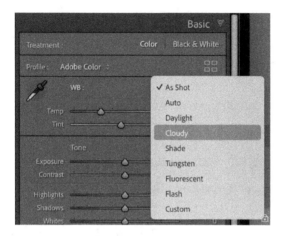

- **Temp (Temperature)**: Adjusts the warmth or coolness of the photo. A positive value will give the image a warm, yellowish tint, while a negative value cools it down, adding blue tones.

- **Tint**: This slider adjusts the green/purple balance. If you're getting an odd color cast from artificial light (say, from fluorescent bulbs), this is the tool you'll use to neutralize it.

I often use the **eyedropper tool** in Lightroom to click on something neutral in the image (like a gray card or white object) to get an automatic white balance adjustment. From there, I tweak it slightly to match the mood I'm after.

Tone Curve Mastery

The **Tone Curve** is where you can refine contrast and tonality with pixel-perfect precision. It's essentially an advanced version of the **Exposure/Contrast sliders**.

- **RGB Curve**: The default curve works with the entire tonal range, allowing you to tweak the brightness of the shadows, midtones, and highlights separately.
- **Channel Curves**: You can also adjust the Red, Green, and Blue channels separately to correct color shifts or create specific color grading effects.

I often use the Tone Curve to create a classic **S-curve** to add contrast. To do this:

1. Click the middle of the curve to anchor it.

2. Pull the shadows down a bit, and the highlights up.

This gives the image more punch without losing details in the shadows or highlights.

Pro Tip: Hold **Shift** while clicking on the Tone Curve to constrain adjustments to just the tonal range you're working with (shadows, midtones, or highlights).

Color Grading with HSL and Color Wheels

Color grading is one of my favorite parts of photo editing, and Lightroom offers a lot of control through **HSL** (Hue, Saturation, Luminance) and **Color Wheels**.

HSL Panel

- **Hue**: Adjusts the color tone. For example, I can make greens look more yellow or more blue.
- **Saturation**: Controls the intensity of colors. You can mute colors (make them less saturated) or punch them up.

- **Luminance**: Affects the brightness of individual colors. For instance, I might want to brighten the reds in a portrait to make skin tones more vibrant, without affecting other areas.

Color Wheels

- The **Color Wheels** panel gives you a powerful way to adjust shadows, midtones, and highlights separately. I use this to give photos a cinematic or moody vibe by adding a subtle tint to shadows or highlights—like a blue tint in the shadows or orange in the highlights.

Sharpening and Noise Reduction

When you're dealing with raw photos, sharpness and noise are often a concern. Lightroom offers great tools for dealing with both.

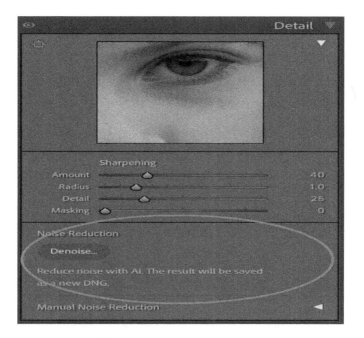

- **Sharpening**: You can adjust the **Amount** of sharpness to bring out fine details in an image, such as textures or hair. Be mindful of the **Radius** and **Detail** sliders to avoid creating unnatural edges.

  I always use **Alt/Option** while dragging the sharpening sliders to see a high-contrast preview of the edges.

- **Noise Reduction**: High-ISO images often introduce noise. Lightroom's **Noise Reduction** feature smooths out grainy areas while preserving detail. The **Luminance** slider works best for reducing noise, while **Color** handles chromatic (color) noise.

Lens Corrections and Transform Tools

Lens distortions (like barrel distortion or chromatic aberration) are a common issue in wide-angle photography, but Lightroom makes it easy to correct them.

- **Lens Corrections**: Lightroom can automatically apply corrections for many lenses (if the lens metadata is available). You can also manually adjust **Distortion** and **Chromatic Aberration** sliders to fix any remaining imperfections.
- **Transform Tools**: I use the **U key** to quickly access the Transform tools. These are incredibly useful for architectural shots,

correcting perspective distortions (like converging lines), and straightening horizons.

Crop, Rotate, and Aspect Ratio Controls

Cropping is the simplest yet most impactful way to improve an image's composition.

The **Crop Overlay Tool** is intuitive:

- Use it to straighten images (by aligning the horizon or vertical lines with the grid) and crop to different aspect ratios (16:9 for landscapes, 4:5 for Instagram posts, etc.).

Tip: Press **R** to quickly toggle between the crop tool and an easy-to-apply grid for alignment.

Mastering the **Develop Module** in Lightroom is about getting comfortable with the tools that transform your raw images into your creative vision. It's an intuitive, non-destructive space where you can experiment, refine, and push the boundaries of what's possible with your photos.

Chapter Six

Advanced Editing Techniques

As an experienced graphic designer, I'm constantly aiming to elevate my images. Lightroom 2025 offers a range of advanced features that allow me to take my editing to the next level. Whether it's isolating a subject for retouching, blending multiple exposures into one seamless image, or creating detailed composites, these tools make it possible to deliver high-quality work.

Local Adjustments: Brush, Gradient, and Radial Filters

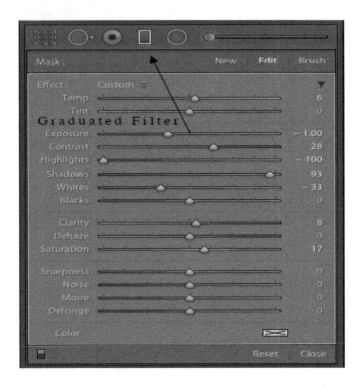

Local adjustments are the bread and butter of detailed photo editing. These tools allow me to target specific areas of an image for precise adjustments, whether it's darkening the background, brightening the subject, or applying a subtle vignette.

Adjustment Brush

The **Adjustment Brush** is my go-to tool for making targeted changes. By simply painting over an area, I can apply changes like:

- Exposure, contrast, or sharpness in specific regions (e.g., brightening a face or adding contrast to shadows under a tree).
- Clarity and texture to emphasize details like skin, hair, or fabrics.
- Selective noise reduction (ideal for smoothing out skin or a blurry background).

Tip: Hold **Alt/Option** to switch from painting to erasing, which helps fine-tune the edges of your brush strokes.

Graduated Filter

The **Graduated Filter** is perfect for landscapes or images with a natural gradient (like a sky transitioning into land). I use it to:

- Gradually adjust exposure, contrast, or clarity across an area (e.g., darkening a bright sky while keeping the landscape perfectly exposed).

- Control the temperature (warm up the foreground or cool down the background for mood).

It's ideal for adding drama to a sunrise or sunset, enhancing the natural light gradient.

Radial Filter

The **Radial Filter** is especially effective for creating a subtle vignette or for isolating the focus of a photo. I use it in several ways:

- Drawing attention to the subject by brightening or sharpening just the center of the frame.
- Adding soft, circular gradients around a face or object (great for portrait work or product photography).
- Creating a blurred background effect (similar to a **depth of field**), which isolates the subject while smoothing the surroundings.

Advanced Masking: Sky, Subject, Background, Object

Lightroom's **Advanced Masking** features are truly a game-changer. Thanks to AI-powered tools, I can now isolate objects, subjects, and even the sky for incredibly precise edits, all without spending hours on manual selections.

Sky Masking

Sky masking is especially useful when editing landscape shots. Lightroom's **AI-powered Sky Masking** detects the sky and allows me to adjust it independently of the rest of the image. I use this to:

- Increase saturation and contrast to make sunsets and sunrises pop.
- Correct color balance (often skies turn unnatural shades due to camera sensor limitations).
- Apply subtle exposure corrections for a more natural look or dramatic mood.

The AI handles clouds, gradients, and transitions beautifully, saving me so much time on complex manual selections.

Subject Masking

Subject masking works similarly but isolates the **main subject** of the image. Whether it's a person, animal, or product, Lightroom's **AI Subject Masking** can detect the edges, making it incredibly easy to:

- Brighten skin tones or adjust contrast and saturation on the subject.
- Apply sharpening and noise reduction only to the subject while leaving the background untouched.

I often use subject masking in portraiture or fashion work to fine-tune the person without affecting the overall environment or scene.

Background Masking

Using **AI Background Masking**, Lightroom now allows me to isolate the background and apply adjustments there as well. This is helpful for:

- Softening a busy background or removing unwanted distractions.
- Decreasing exposure or applying a blur effect to create better subject isolation.

It's perfect for improving depth of field or creating separation between a subject and a cluttered background without needing to jump into Photoshop.

Object Masking

For intricate selections like product photography or interior shots, **AI Object Masking** is a lifesaver. Lightroom's AI can detect specific objects and mask them, making it easy to:

- Adjust the brightness, contrast, and color of individual items in a complex scene (e.g., brightening a product or enhancing texture in an object without altering the background).

- Correct imperfections like reflections or lighting inconsistencies on objects.

I love using this feature for commercial product shoots where accuracy and detail are paramount.

Merging HDR and Panoramas

Sometimes, a single photo just can't capture the full dynamic range or sweeping vistas I'm after. This is where **HDR (High Dynamic Range)** and **Panorama** stitching come in.

Merging HDR

HDR photography allows me to capture images with extreme light variations, like sunset or interior shots with both bright windows and dark shadows. Lightroom 2025 offers a fantastic **HDR Merge** feature that:

- Combines multiple exposures (usually 3-7 images with varying exposure levels) into a single image.
- Corrects tone and color, ensuring the final image looks natural and balanced.

This tool is indispensable when I'm photographing interiors or landscapes with varying lighting conditions.

Tip: Use the **Auto Tone** option after merging HDR images to balance exposure across all parts of the image before fine-tuning the colors and contrast.

Panorama Merge

Panorama Merging allows me to seamlessly stitch together multiple images into a wide-angle or ultra-wide shot. I use this when I'm capturing:

- Vast landscapes that I want to capture in their full glory.
- Architectural scenes that require a wide view.

It's effortless—just select the images, and Lightroom handles the stitching, blending, and adjusting for lens distortion. After the merge, I can refine the image with all the tools Lightroom offers, including cropping and transforming.

Mastering **Advanced Editing Techniques** in Lightroom 2025 gives me full creative control over my images. With the combination of AI-powered masking, local adjustments, and the ability to merge multiple shots into a single stunning composition, I can create images that truly stand out.

Each tool serves a purpose, whether I'm doing subtle refinements or large-scale edits. The beauty of Lightroom is that it offers a non-destructive, flexible environment where I can experiment freely and always know I can undo a change if I need to.

Creating and Using Custom Presets

As a graphic designer, I'm all about efficiency without sacrificing creativity. **Custom Presets** are a huge time-saver in Lightroom because they allow me to save specific settings (like exposure, contrast, color grading, etc.) and apply them to any image with just one click. Here's how I approach creating and using them:

Why Custom Presets Are Essential

Presets allow me to maintain a consistent style across a series of images. Whether I'm editing a batch of product photos, a fashion shoot, or a landscape series, using the same preset helps ensure that all images have a uniform aesthetic. I create my own presets based on:

- My editing style (warm, cool, moody, etc.).
- The type of images I'm working on (portraits, landscapes, interiors, etc.).

- My go-to adjustments (shadows, highlights, sharpness, color grading).

How to Create a Custom Preset

1. **Make your adjustments**: Start by adjusting a single image to the desired look—exposure, contrast, sharpening, color grading, etc.

2. **Save the settings**: On the left panel in the **Develop Module**, click the + next to the **Presets** section, then choose **Create Preset**.

3. **Choose the settings**: Lightroom will allow you to select which specific adjustments you want to include in the preset (e.g., exposure, contrast, tone curve, etc.). I recommend only including the adjustments that will be consistent across all photos.

4. **Name and organize**: Give your preset a clear name (e.g., "Warm Portraits" or "Moody Landscape") and organize it into a group if needed.

5. **Apply your preset**: To apply the preset to other images, simply select the image, then

click the preset name under the **Presets** panel.

Tip: When working on a batch of images from a single shoot, apply the same preset to all of them to quickly bring consistency. You can always tweak individual images later.

Using Presets for Different Projects

For different types of work, I create several presets tailored to specific styles:

- **Portraits**: A preset for skin tone enhancements, softening, and minor exposure tweaks.
- **Landscapes**: A preset for increased clarity, vibrance, and saturation of the sky and foreground.
- **Black and White**: A preset that enhances contrast and texture for a striking monochrome effect.

Having these on hand saves me tons of time, especially when editing large projects like wedding albums, portfolios, or real estate photos.

Working with LUTs and Color Profiles

In Lightroom 2025, **LUTs (Look-Up Tables)** and **color profiles** offer advanced ways to control the colors and overall aesthetic of my images. These tools allow me to go beyond simple adjustments and dive deep into color grading for a cinematic or unique look.

What Are LUTs and Color Profiles?

- **LUTs (Look-Up Tables)** are essentially preset color transformations that adjust the color balance of an image. They're commonly used in video editing but can be applied to photos as well. They map one set of colors to another, allowing me to add mood or stylized color schemes quickly. For example, a LUT can make an image look like it was shot during golden hour or apply a vintage film effect.

- **Color Profiles** are predefined sets of colors that adjust the color space of an image. They're often used to give a consistent look to a series of images or to match the output of a specific camera or lens.

How to Use LUTs in Lightroom

1. **Install LUTs**: You can download LUTs from external sources, or Lightroom comes with a set of basic LUTs. To install third-party LUTs, I simply drag them into the **LUTs** folder in the **Develop Module** (or use the **Profile Browser**).

2. **Apply a LUT**: In the **Develop Module**, go to the **Profile** section (just below the Basic Panel) and click **Browse**. From here, I can select a LUT or browse custom LUTs I've installed.

3. **Fine-tune the LUT**: Once a LUT is applied, I can tweak the intensity of the effect using the **Amount** slider. This allows me to dial the effect up or down to suit the photo's look and feel.

4. **Experiment with multiple LUTs**: For more creative control, I apply multiple LUTs in combination, layering them for unique effects.

Tip: I often combine LUTs with other adjustments (like exposure or contrast) to fine-tune the final look. I can also use the **Color Grading** panel after applying a LUT to further manipulate the shadows, midtones, and highlights.

Using Color Profiles

Color profiles offer more control over the overall look and feel of an image. Lightroom provides several built-in profiles like **Adobe Color**, **Adobe Monochrome**, **Camera Matching**, and others. Here's how I use them:

1. **Choosing a Profile**: In the **Develop Module**, I select a profile in the **Profile** dropdown. If I'm aiming for a specific look, I select one from the **Creative** section. For example, **Adobe Landscape** enhances the vibrancy

and contrast, making it perfect for nature shots.

2. **Fine-tuning the Profile**: Just like LUTs, I can adjust the strength of the color profile using the **Amount** slider to dial the effect back or apply it fully.

3. **Custom Profiles**: If I'm working on a specific camera, I might use the **Camera Matching** profile, which is designed to match the colors of that camera's default settings.

Tip: I use **Adobe Standard** when I want a neutral, unaltered base profile that I can further customize for my specific look.

Why Combine LUTs and Color Profiles?

Combining LUTs and color profiles is a fantastic way to create unique, consistent looks across multiple images. For example, I might start with a **Camera Matching Profile** to give me a base color range, then layer on a **LUT** for a stylized effect (such as a film look or cinematic mood).

By pairing both tools, I gain even more creative freedom to manipulate color and tone, achieving the exact vibe I'm after.

Creating and Using Custom Presets and **Working with LUTs and Color Profiles** are some of the most efficient and creative tools available in Lightroom. As a professional, these features help me maintain consistency across my projects while also offering endless possibilities for customizations. Whether I'm building a preset for a client, experimenting with color grading for artistic shots, or quickly applying a cinematic LUT to a landscape, Lightroom makes it incredibly easy to deliver high-quality, polished work in less time.

Chapter Seven

Workflow and File Management

Whether I'm working on a large batch of photos or just a few carefully curated images, maintaining a solid workflow is essential to avoid chaos and confusion. Lightroom's powerful tools make organizing, editing, and managing my images both intuitive and effective. Here's how I handle the process from start to finish.

Creating a Non-Destructive Editing Workflow

One of the things I love about Lightroom is its **non-destructive** approach to editing. Unlike Photoshop, where edits are permanent unless you explicitly save them, Lightroom keeps all adjustments stored separately from the original file. This ensures that I can always revert to my original image if needed, which is a huge relief when experimenting with edits or trying new techniques.

How It Works

- **Non-Destructive Editing**: When I import photos into Lightroom, the software creates a catalog of the images, and any edits I make are stored as metadata. This means that the original file is never altered. I can always go back and re-edit or reset any adjustments without affecting the original image.

- **History Panel**: I use the **History Panel** in the **Develop Module** to keep track of every edit I make. Each step is recorded, so I can jump back to any point in my editing process.

- **Snapshots**: I use **Snapshots** to capture specific points in my editing workflow. If I like a particular look but want to continue experimenting, I can take a snapshot and return to that look whenever I want. This way, I never have to worry about losing the progress I liked during the editing process.

Working with Virtual Copies

If I need to create variations of an image, such as testing out different edits or applying multiple presets, I use **Virtual Copies**. These are exact duplicates of my original photo within Lightroom that allow me to experiment freely without creating extra files. Once I'm happy with one version, I can export it as needed, and the original file remains untouched.

Tip: I create **virtual copies** for client work, where I may need to send them a few options of a shot. It's all done within the same catalog, which keeps things organized and simple.

Syncing Lightroom Across Devices

As a graphic designer, I work from multiple devices, including my desktop and laptop, and occasionally my tablet when I'm on the go. Lightroom's **cloud syncing** capabilities make this an easy process, ensuring that my work is seamlessly integrated and accessible across devices.

Lightroom Desktop and Mobile Sync

Lightroom allows me to sync my images and edits across multiple platforms using Adobe's cloud service. Here's how I manage it:

1. **Cloud Sync**: I ensure that the images I import into Lightroom are stored in the cloud. This way, they're accessible from my desktop, laptop, or mobile devices, making it easy to work on the go.

2. **Editing Anywhere**: Once my images are synced, I can open and edit them on my mobile device through **Lightroom Mobile**. This is perfect when I'm traveling or working remotely. All my edits are synced automatically, and when I open Lightroom back on my desktop, the changes are reflected.

3. **Smart Previews**: If I'm on a slow connection or want to conserve bandwidth, I can use **Smart Previews** to sync

lower-resolution versions of my images. This way, I can still make edits on my mobile device or laptop without using the full-resolution files.

Tip: To save on storage, I use Lightroom's **Sync Settings** to decide which photos get synced and which ones stay local. For instance, I sync only the images I need for active projects, while the rest stay on my desktop for organization.

Benefits of Cloud Syncing

- **Continuity**: Whether I'm at my desk or on the move, my editing workflow stays consistent. I never have to worry about carrying all my files or worrying if I'm missing an important image.
- **Client Proofing**: The cloud integration makes it easy to send images for client review. I can sync my photos to **Lightroom Web**, where clients can view and leave feedback directly on the images.

Backing Up Your Lightroom Catalog

When it comes to managing my Lightroom catalog, **backups** are a must. As a professional, losing my work would be catastrophic, especially when I'm handling large projects for clients or personal portfolio work. Lightroom makes it easy to back up my catalog and ensure my images are safe.

Backing Up the Catalog

The **Lightroom Catalog** holds all of my edits, metadata, and organizational structures. It's crucial that I back up this catalog regularly to avoid losing any work. Here's how I do it:

1. **Auto-Backups**: I set Lightroom to back up my catalog automatically. I usually choose to back it up every time I close Lightroom. This ensures that I always have the latest version of my catalog saved.

2. **Manual Backups**: On top of auto-backups, I also perform manual backups, especially before major changes or large projects. I store my backups on a separate external hard

drive, as well as in the cloud for extra
security.

Backing Up Images

In addition to catalog backups, I also back up my
original image files. Lightroom's non-destructive
nature means the edits are saved in the catalog, but
the images themselves should be backed up too.

1. **External Storage**: I always store my raw
   files and exports on an external hard drive,
   using a reliable drive with plenty of space.
2. **Cloud Storage**: For redundancy, I use cloud
   storage services (like Adobe Cloud,
   Dropbox, or Google Drive) for extra peace
   of mind. I keep my current projects synced
   to the cloud so I can access them from
   anywhere, and if my local drive fails, I know
   I have a backup.

Tip: Follow the **3-2-1 rule** for backups: 3 copies of
your data (1 original, 2 backups), 2 different types
of media (external hard drive, cloud), and 1 off-site

copy (cloud backup). This gives me the highest level of protection against data loss.

Restore a Catalog

If something goes wrong and I need to restore my catalog, Lightroom makes it simple:

- I go to **File > Open Catalog** and select the most recent backup.
- Lightroom will prompt me to overwrite my current catalog, or I can choose to open the backup as a new catalog.

Tip: I always keep at least 3 catalog backups before deleting older versions. That way, if I encounter an issue with a recent backup, I can go back to an earlier one.

Efficient **Workflow and File Management** in Lightroom is crucial for maintaining productivity and ensuring my images are safe. By leveraging Lightroom's **non-destructive editing** workflow, **cloud syncing** capabilities, and comprehensive **backup strategies**, I can confidently manage my projects from start to finish, knowing that my files are organized, easily accessible, and secure.

Whether I'm syncing images across multiple devices, backing up my catalog, or editing on the go, Lightroom's tools make managing my workflow and files a breeze.

Exporting Images for Print, Web, and Social Media

When it comes to **exporting images**, Lightroom provides a robust set of tools that allow me to prepare images for various platforms and formats. Depending on the final output, I tweak my export settings to ensure my images look their best, whether I'm printing them, uploading them to a website, or sharing them on social media.

1. Exporting for Print

As a graphic designer, I often print images for clients, exhibitions, or portfolios. **Print-quality images** require the highest possible resolution and color accuracy. Here's how I approach printing exports:

Print Settings

1. **Resolution**: When preparing images for print, I always export at a resolution of **300 DPI** (dots per inch). This ensures the image is sharp and suitable for large prints without any pixelation.

2. **Color Space**: For print, I select the **Adobe RGB (1998)** color space. This provides a wider range of colors and is commonly used in professional printing.

3. **File Format**: I usually export as **TIFF** or **JPEG**. TIFF is preferred for high-quality prints, while JPEG can be used for less demanding jobs (though I always choose the highest quality setting for the best results).

4. **Sharpening**: I use the **Standard** setting in the **Sharpening for Output** options, as it balances detail without over-sharpening the image.

5. **Metadata**: If I'm printing for a client, I sometimes choose to include the **metadata** so they know about the image's origin, camera settings, and more.

Example Settings for Print:

- File Format: TIFF or JPEG
- Color Space: Adobe RGB (1998)
- Resolution: 300 DPI
- Output Sharpening: Standard
- Include Metadata: Optional, based on client preference

Tip: Before exporting, I make sure to soft-proof the image using the **Print Preview** to simulate how the colors will appear when printed. This helps catch any color discrepancies between my monitor and the printer.

2. Exporting for the Web

Web images have a different set of requirements. They need to be optimized for quick loading times without sacrificing too much quality. Here's how I optimize images for the web:

Web Settings

1. **Resolution**: For web use, I usually stick to **72 DPI** since higher resolutions won't provide any benefit for online viewing.

2. **File Format**: **JPEG** is usually my go-to file format for web images. It strikes a good balance between file size and image quality. For transparent images (like logos or icons), I opt for **PNG**.

3. **Quality**: I set the **Quality** slider to around **80-85%** to ensure the file size is small without noticeable loss in quality.

4. **Resize**: I often resize images to specific dimensions based on the website's requirements (e.g., 1200px wide for blog images). This ensures that images are optimized for display without taking up too much space.

5. **Sharpening**: I use the **Low** or **Standard** output sharpening for web exports. This ensures the image still looks sharp on a variety of screens without introducing any excessive noise.

Example Settings for Web:

- File Format: JPEG or PNG
- Resolution: 72 DPI
- Quality: 80-85%
- Resize: Custom dimensions (based on web needs)
- Sharpening: Standard or Low

Tip: When exporting for social media, I make sure the file dimensions match the recommended sizes for each platform. For example, Instagram images should typically be 1080px wide, while Facebook images may need to be resized to 2048px wide for the best display.

3. Exporting for Social Media

Social media platforms have specific requirements to ensure the best image quality. To streamline my process, I follow a similar approach to web export but with adjustments for each platform's needs.

Social Media Settings

1. **File Format**: I stick to **JPEG** because it's widely accepted across all social platforms and offers a good balance of quality and file size.

2. **Resolution**: I export at **72 DPI** for quick loading times and small file sizes.

3. **File Size**: Platforms like Instagram and Facebook have file size limits (typically under 20MB), so I make sure to optimize the image to fit within these limits.

4. **Resize**: Each social platform has its own optimal image size. For instance:
   - **Instagram**: 1080px (square) or 1350px (portrait)
   - **Facebook**: 2048px (wide)
   - **Twitter**: 1200px (wide)
   - **LinkedIn**: 1200px (wide)

5. **Sharpening**: Social media images often look softer after compression, so I use **Standard** sharpening to compensate for this.

Example Settings for Social Media:

- File Format: JPEG
- Resolution: 72 DPI
- Quality: 80-90%
- Resize: Specific to platform (e.g., 1080px for Instagram)
- Sharpening: Standard or High

Tip: Always preview your images on the platform before posting. Each platform has its own compression algorithm, and the final result might differ slightly from what you see in Lightroom. Some platforms can even strip metadata, so ensure no essential information is lost.

Integrating with Photoshop and Other Adobe Apps

As an experienced designer, I'm frequently bouncing between Adobe's suite of tools, and Lightroom seamlessly integrates with **Photoshop** and other Adobe apps like **Adobe Camera Raw**, **Adobe Illustrator**, and **Adobe Photoshop Express**. This integration streamlines my workflow, allowing me to leverage the strengths of each program without breaking my creative flow.

1. Integrating Lightroom with Photoshop

One of the main reasons I love using Lightroom is its tight integration with **Photoshop**. When an image needs more advanced editing than Lightroom's tools can provide (e.g., detailed retouching, complex composites, or creative filters), I can send it directly to Photoshop without needing to export or duplicate the file.

Editing in Photoshop from Lightroom

1. **Send an Image to Photoshop**: Once my image is edited in Lightroom, I simply right-click on the image in the **Library** or **Develop** module and select **Edit in Photoshop**. The image will open in Photoshop, and I can perform any advanced edits I need.

2. **Round-Trip Editing**: After making adjustments in Photoshop, I can **save** the file and automatically return to Lightroom. The

image appears as a new file in the catalog (called a **TIFF** or **PSD**, depending on my settings).

3. **Non-Destructive Workflow**: Just like in Lightroom, Photoshop edits are non-destructive when I work with **smart objects**. This allows me to go back and make changes without altering the original file.

Tip: I often use Photoshop for tasks like adding text, creating complex composites, or fine-tuning skin tones, then bring it back into Lightroom for final color grading and export.

2. Lightroom and Adobe Camera Raw (ACR)

Adobe Camera Raw (ACR) is another powerhouse that works seamlessly with Lightroom. If I need to open raw files from Lightroom directly into Photoshop, Camera Raw is often used as the bridge. It provides the same adjustment tools as Lightroom, so I can apply edits in one and continue seamlessly in the other.

3. Integrating with Adobe Illustrator and Photoshop Express

For graphic design projects, **Adobe Illustrator** is my go-to for vector-based work like logos, typography, and illustrations. I often import high-resolution images from Lightroom into Illustrator for use in designs and layouts.

- **Photoshop Express** is another app I use on my mobile device. It's great for quick edits when I'm away from my desktop, and it syncs with Lightroom so I can access and edit my images on the go.

Exporting Images for Print, Web, and Social Media and **Integrating with Photoshop and Other Adobe Apps** are essential parts of my workflow. With Lightroom's powerful export tools, I can ensure that my images are optimized for any output, whether it's a high-quality print, a social media post, or a web gallery. And with seamless integration with other Adobe apps, I can push my creative vision even further, knowing that all my tools work together in perfect harmony.

Chapter Eight

Mobile & Cloud Features

With **Lightroom 2025**, Adobe has taken mobile and cloud features to the next level, integrating everything seamlessly to allow professionals to stay productive no matter where they are. Whether you're editing on your phone, tablet, or desktop, Lightroom's mobile and cloud tools ensure that your images are always accessible and editable in real-time.

1. Lightroom Mobile: Editing on the Go

As someone who works across different environments—from client meetings to outdoor shoots—it's important for me to be able to edit my images anywhere, anytime. **Lightroom Mobile** gives me that flexibility and is just as powerful as the desktop version, with the added benefit of portability.

The Power of Lightroom Mobile

- **Full Editing Capabilities**: Even though Lightroom Mobile is on a smaller screen, it offers most of the essential editing tools that are available in the desktop version. You can make global adjustments (exposure, contrast, white balance, etc.), apply local adjustments (brush, gradient, radial filters), and even use advanced features like **AI-powered masking** and **generative fill**.

- **Touch and Gesture Controls**: Editing on a tablet or smartphone feels intuitive thanks to Lightroom's responsive touch interface. Pinch-to-zoom, swipe to adjust sliders, and tap to toggle between tools—these gestures allow me to work quickly and precisely.

- **RAW Editing**: Lightroom Mobile supports **RAW files**, which is essential for maintaining the highest quality in my work. Whether I shoot in RAW on my camera or use my phone's advanced camera features, Lightroom Mobile lets me process these files with all the same flexibility I get on desktop.

- **Syncing Between Devices**: Any edits I make on Lightroom Mobile sync across all my devices, thanks to Adobe's cloud-based ecosystem. This means that I can start editing a batch of photos on my phone during my commute, then continue refining them on my desktop later without missing a beat.

Use Cases for Lightroom Mobile

- **Travel and On-the-Go Workflows**: When I'm traveling for work, I often shoot on location, and Lightroom Mobile lets me do quick edits while still capturing the atmosphere. I can send my final edited images to clients or upload them to social media without needing my laptop.
- **Client Reviews**: I use Lightroom Mobile to show clients drafts and concepts while on-site. The mobile version is a fantastic way to get quick feedback without lugging around a heavy laptop.

Tip: If you shoot a lot of portrait or landscape photos, Lightroom Mobile's **crop and straighten** tools come in handy, especially when I need to adjust framing while I'm out on location.

2. Cloud Storage and Auto Backup

The convenience of cloud storage has taken my workflow efficiency to another level. With **Adobe Cloud**, I no longer worry about manually backing up photos or losing important files. Everything I work on, from edits to exports, is automatically synced across all my devices and backed up securely.

Benefits of Lightroom's Cloud Storage

- **Seamless Syncing**: All images, edits, and metadata sync to the cloud. This means whether I'm editing on my desktop, mobile device, or laptop, everything is always up-to-date. I don't have to worry about manually transferring files between devices.
- **Smart Storage**: Lightroom's cloud storage automatically selects images that are most

important or recent, ensuring I don't run out of space. It also offers **50GB or 1TB** storage options, depending on my plan.

- **Auto Backup**: My images are safely stored and backed up in the cloud as I work. This auto-backup feature gives me peace of mind, knowing that I'm not risking losing months of work due to a crashed hard drive or lost file.

Efficient Cloud Management

- **Automatic Sync**: Lightroom's automatic syncing means that whenever I import new photos or make changes to existing ones, they're instantly backed up to the cloud and accessible from any of my devices.
- **Cloud Storage Access**: As someone who works on a variety of devices, being able to access my photos from anywhere, whether it's on my phone or laptop, is a huge advantage. I can continue editing at home, on the go, or even on the job site, as long as I have an internet connection.

- **Sharing**: Cloud storage also enables easy sharing of files with clients or collaborators. I can create **shared albums** or **publish galleries**, allowing others to access images in real-time without needing to send large files via email or FTP.

Backup for Peace of Mind

- **Local and Cloud Copies**: Even though my photos are synced to the cloud, I still make sure to have a local copy of my most important work on a hard drive or external storage device. I tend to save high-resolution versions of my projects locally and keep edits and raw files safely stored on the cloud.

Tip: Lightroom allows me to **choose whether images are stored locally** or **in the cloud**. For projects that require maximum space-saving, I keep only the important edits in the cloud and store high-res versions locally or on an external hard drive. This helps me manage space without worrying about losing data.

3. Collaborative Features

Lightroom Mobile and Cloud aren't just about personal convenience—they also open the door for more **collaborative workflows**. If I'm working on a project with a team, Lightroom's cloud storage and sharing features make collaboration a breeze.

- **Shared Albums**: I can invite clients or collaborators to view images in real time. They can make comments on the photos, or I can create a shared album where they can download or comment on different versions.
- **Live Edits**: As I edit, the changes reflect instantly on all devices connected to the cloud. This is especially useful when working on client reviews or multi-team collaborations.

Tip: For clients with specific editing needs, I create shared collections in Lightroom and share direct links to those collections, allowing clients to view edits without needing Lightroom installed on their device.

The **Mobile and Cloud Features** of Lightroom 2025 have made my life as a designer and photographer much easier. Whether I'm editing on the go with **Lightroom Mobile** or ensuring all my images are safely backed up and synced with **Adobe Cloud**, these features give me the flexibility and security I need. I can seamlessly switch between devices, collaborate with clients in real time, and always know that my images are safe, organized, and ready to be shared or exported.

Shared Albums and Collaboration Tools

One of the best aspects of Lightroom is its ability to facilitate collaboration with clients, teams, and colleagues. In my line of work, efficient collaboration can make all the difference, whether I'm working with a photographer, fellow designer, or a client with specific requests.

1. Creating and Managing Shared Albums

Lightroom allows me to **create shared albums** that can be accessed by others. This is ideal for sharing images with clients for review, working with collaborators on a project, or curating portfolios for exhibitions.

How to Create a Shared Album

1. **Create an Album**: In Lightroom's **Library Module**, I create an album by selecting the images I want to group and organizing them into a new album. I name it based on the project or client, making it easy to keep track of different groups of photos.

2. **Share the Album**: Once the album is set, I click on the **Share icon** at the top right of the album panel. I can choose to share the album with specific people via an **invitation link** or **directly through email**.

3. **Permission Control**: I can set permissions to decide whether recipients can only view or also contribute images. If I want clients to only view the images and leave comments, I set the permission to **View Only**. On the other hand, if the project is collaborative, I can give permission to **Upload** images.

4. **URL for Easy Sharing**: Lightroom also generates a **unique URL** that I can send to

anyone who needs access. This makes sharing quick and seamless, without worrying about large attachments or email size restrictions.

Using Shared Albums for Collaboration

- **Client Feedback**: I often share albums with clients for quick feedback. The client can view the images, leave comments directly on individual photos, and even select their favorite images. This keeps all feedback in one place, making it easier to track revisions.

- **Team Collaboration**: When working with a team, such as a photographer or another designer, I can easily share my work in progress, so they can contribute edits or provide feedback. We can go back and forth quickly without the need for constant emails or file exchanges.

Real-Time Updates

The best part is that when I make edits to any of the shared images, they update in real-time. This is especially useful when I'm working with a team, as they can see the changes instantly and adjust their work accordingly.

Tip: If I'm working on a large project with many clients or team members, I organize shared albums by project or deliverable. This keeps everything neat and ensures I can easily track and manage all feedback.

2. Commenting and Feedback Tools

When sharing albums with clients or collaborators, **commenting** becomes an invaluable feature. Each photo in a shared album has a **comment section** where stakeholders can leave feedback, suggest edits, or approve certain images.

How I Use Commenting

- **Detailed Feedback**: If a client is unsure about a particular aspect of an image (say, the color grading or composition), they can leave a detailed comment directly on that image. This makes it easier for me to understand exactly what changes need to be made.

- **Approval and Rejection**: Clients can flag images they love by liking them, while images they don't want can be marked for rejection. This allows me to quickly identify which images to work on further and which ones are already approved.

Tip: I find that keeping a **"Notes"** album dedicated to client or team feedback helps organize all the comments. I can easily look back at the feedback without searching through individual images.

Lightroom Web Version Features

With the **Lightroom Web Version**, Adobe has expanded its reach and given me the ability to work on my photos, edit them, and manage my collections, all from a browser. This means that no matter where I am—whether on the go or at a coffee shop with my laptop—I can access my Lightroom library and continue my editing workflow.

1. Full Access to Lightroom Library

The web version of Lightroom offers near-full access to my **Lightroom catalog** and everything stored in my **cloud library**. I can **view** and **organize** images, create collections, and even apply basic edits without needing the desktop app.

What's Available on Lightroom Web

- **Image Viewing and Rating**: Just like the desktop version, I can view my images, rate them, flag them, or label them according to their status (e.g., "needs editing," "finalized," etc.).
- **Albums and Collections**: The web version supports the **albums** and **collections** that I've created on the desktop app. I can add or remove images from albums and collections with ease, keeping everything organized.
- **Cloud Syncing**: Any changes made on the web automatically sync with the desktop and

mobile versions of Lightroom, ensuring I always have the latest updates across all devices.

2. Basic Editing Tools

While the web version doesn't offer all the advanced editing capabilities found in the desktop app, it does provide essential editing tools for quick adjustments. These are great when I'm on the move and don't have access to my full workstation.

Editing on the Web

- **Basic Adjustments**: I can adjust **exposure**, **contrast**, **highlights**, and **shadows**. Lightroom Web also provides **crop** and **straighten** tools to help fine-tune compositions.
- **Presets**: I can apply my **custom presets** from the desktop version in Lightroom Web, allowing me to maintain consistency across my images while on the go.
- **AI-powered Features**: Lightroom Web includes access to some **AI tools** like **Auto**

Adjustments, which automatically enhance my photos based on Adobe's machine learning algorithms.

Photo Sharing on the Web

- **Instant Sharing**: One of the best features of the web version is the ability to share images with clients, collaborators, or anyone else via a **direct link**. I can share individual photos or entire albums, and the recipients don't need to have Lightroom installed—they just need a web browser.

Tip: For collaborative projects, I use the web version to quickly share high-resolution proofs with clients for feedback before I move into more detailed edits. This allows me to keep the process fast and efficient.

3. Cross-Platform Syncing

Lightroom Web seamlessly integrates with the **Lightroom mobile** and **desktop versions**, ensuring that my entire library is accessible no matter where I am or what device I'm using. Whether I'm at home, in the office, or out on a shoot, I can pick up right where I left off.

- **Sync from Mobile**: If I upload photos directly from my mobile device, they are instantly available on the web version. Any edits or changes made on my phone are automatically synced to the web and desktop versions, maintaining continuity across devices.
- **Seamless Workflow**: I never have to worry about losing my edits or having to export and import between devices. Everything stays in sync across the Lightroom ecosystem.

Tip: When I need to quickly organize or delete photos after a shoot, the web version is a great tool for making these quick decisions without having to be tethered to my desktop.

The **Shared Albums and Collaboration Tools** in Lightroom, paired with the **web version**, are incredibly powerful features for anyone in the creative field. These tools allow me to share work, get feedback, and collaborate with clients and teams in real time. Whether it's creating albums for client reviews or using the web version to make quick adjustments on the go, Lightroom has truly streamlined my workflow.

With the cloud-based features and seamless syncing across platforms, I can manage my entire photography and design process, from import to export, no matter where I am or what device I'm using. These features make Lightroom not just a tool, but a central hub for my creative work.

Chapter Nine

Creative Projects and Productivity

Lightroom isn't just about photo editing—it's a comprehensive creative tool that helps me bring my projects to life, whether for personal use, clients, or professional portfolios. Whether I need to create something for a client presentation or compile a personal portfolio, the **Creative Projects** and **Productivity** tools in Lightroom provide me with all the resources I need to keep the creative process flowing.

1. Creating Slideshows and Photo Books

Sometimes, a photo is just the beginning of a creative project. In Lightroom, I can take my images beyond static photos and turn them into **slideshows** or **photo books**—two great ways to present my work in an engaging and polished way.

Creating a Slideshow

The **Slideshow Module** in Lightroom is an easy and effective way to showcase a set of images in a visually appealing way. I use it frequently when I need to present a collection of photos for a client or even create personal projects like photo highlights from a recent shoot.

How to Create a Slideshow in Lightroom

1. **Select Images**: First, I choose the images I want to showcase. This could be a curated set of photos from a shoot, or a portfolio of work I want to display.

2. **Customize the Slideshow**: Lightroom allows me to customize the **layout**, **transitions**, and **timing** of each slide. I can adjust the **duration of each image** on screen, choose transitions between slides (such as fades or wipes), and even add **background music** to complement the flow of the slideshow.

3. **Export or Present**: Once my slideshow is complete, I can **export it as a video file** or **present it directly** within Lightroom. Exporting is great for sharing with clients or on social media, while presenting within

Lightroom is ideal for in-person presentations or meetings.

Tip: I often use Lightroom's **Ken Burns effect** for creating smooth, subtle motion within slideshows. This effect is perfect for adding dynamic movement to a still image, making the slideshow feel more engaging.

Creating a Photo Book

Photo books are an excellent way to present a set of images in a tangible, beautifully-designed format. With Lightroom's **Book Module**, I can create everything from professional portfolios to personal photo albums. The best part is that it integrates seamlessly with **Blurb**, a popular photo book printing service, allowing me to print high-quality physical books directly from Lightroom.

How to Create a Photo Book in Lightroom

1. **Select Images**: As with slideshows, I start by selecting the photos I want to include in my book. These can be from different

collections, albums, or even individual images.

2. **Design the Layout**: The **Book Module** provides a range of templates to choose from, or I can create my own custom layout. I can drag and drop photos into predefined templates or position them freely on each page. I also have control over **font types**, **text size**, and **spacing**—perfect for adding captions or titles.

3. **Order and Print**: Once the design is ready, I can directly order my book from **Blurb**. Lightroom also gives me the option to export the book as a PDF if I prefer to print it elsewhere. This feature has saved me countless hours in designing personalized albums or portfolio books for clients.

Tip: I make use of Lightroom's **automatic page layouts**, which speed up the book-making process. If I'm on a tight deadline, I let Lightroom auto-arrange my images and then customize the layout from there.

2. Batch Editing and Time-Saving Tricks

One of Lightroom's standout features is its ability to handle large volumes of images efficiently. **Batch editing** is one of the most powerful tools for speeding up my workflow, especially when dealing with multiple images from the same shoot or project. Whether I'm working on a wedding shoot, a product photoshoot, or a series of portraits, batch editing helps me process multiple images in just a few clicks.

Batch Editing: The Basics

Batch editing allows me to apply the same settings to multiple images at once. This can save me a lot of time when I'm editing large sets of images that share similar characteristics. Here's how I use it:

How to Apply Batch Edits

1. **Select Multiple Images**: In the **Library Module**, I select the images I want to apply edits to. These can be from the same shoot or a series of photos with similar lighting, composition, and color tones.

2. **Sync Settings**: After making adjustments to one image, I can apply those same adjustments to the selected images. To do this, I click the **Sync** button in the bottom right of the Develop Module. Lightroom will then copy the settings (exposure, contrast, color grading, etc.) and apply them to all selected images.

3. **Fine-Tune Adjustments**: After syncing, I can go back and fine-tune the edits for individual images if needed. For example, if some images are brighter than others, I can make slight adjustments without having to redo the whole batch.

Tip: I often use **virtual copies** when experimenting with different edits for a series of images. This allows me to quickly try multiple looks without altering the original image.

Time-Saving Tricks

In addition to batch editing, there are several tricks I use to make my workflow even faster:

- **Use Presets**: Presets are a huge time-saver in my workflow. By saving my common adjustments (such as color grading, exposure tweaks, or black-and-white conversion), I can apply them with a single click.

- **Auto Sync**: When I need to apply the same adjustments across a whole batch, I use **Auto Sync** in the Develop Module. Once activated, any edits I make to one image automatically apply to all selected images, which is perfect for maintaining consistency across a set of photos.

- **Copy-Paste Edits**: If I have an image with ideal settings, I can simply **copy the settings** (Ctrl/Cmd + C) and then **paste** them onto another image (Ctrl/Cmd + V). This method is perfect for quick edits when you don't need to sync entire batches.

- **Import Presets for Speed**: I apply **import presets** to automatically adjust images when they come into Lightroom. For example, I have a preset for landscape shots that automatically adjusts the contrast and saturation as soon as the photos are imported, saving me time in post-processing.

Tip: **Batch renaming** is another trick I use when working with large projects. Lightroom lets me rename multiple images during import or after, making file organization a breeze.

The **Creative Projects** and **Productivity** features in Lightroom 2025 are essential for boosting creativity and saving time. Whether I'm creating an impressive slideshow for a client presentation, designing a personalized photo book, or speeding up my editing with batch processing, Lightroom offers everything I need to get the job done efficiently without sacrificing quality.

By making full use of **batch editing** and **creative project tools**, I can focus more on the creative aspects of my work and less on the tedious tasks. And with features like **Slideshow** and **Photo Book creation**, I can easily present my work in ways that leave a lasting impression on my clients or audience.

Automating Workflows with Smart Presets

One of the standout features in **Lightroom 2025** is its ability to automate complex workflows through the use of **Smart Presets**. These presets allow me to set up customized adjustments that apply automatically, saving me time and ensuring consistency across my projects. Whether I'm working on a series of photos or handling a high-volume shoot, **Smart Presets** let me streamline my editing process without sacrificing quality.

What Are Smart Presets?

Smart Presets are presets that go beyond simple, one-click adjustments. They can incorporate more dynamic features, like **conditional editing**, where certain edits are applied based on the image content. For instance, I can create a preset that adjusts the exposure and white balance based on the lighting conditions or camera settings, or one that applies specific color grading to portrait photos but not to landscapes. These presets are designed to adapt to each photo's unique characteristics, making them a powerful tool for automating edits without being one-size-fits-all.

How to Set Up Smart Presets in Lightroom

1. **Create a New Preset**: Start by making a standard preset using Lightroom's regular editing tools in the **Develop Module**. Adjust exposure, contrast, color grading, etc., until you're satisfied with the settings.

2. **Add Conditional Adjustments**: For more advanced automation, I use Lightroom's **masking and AI features** to create condition-based rules. For example, I can build a preset that automatically applies **AI masking** to subjects or skies, making sure the edits only affect the parts of the image I want.

3. **Save and Apply**: Once my Smart Preset is ready, I save it. Lightroom will now automatically apply these settings whenever I import new images that match the preset's conditions.

How I Use Smart Presets in My Workflow

As a professional, I often work with large sets of images—be it for a client project or a personal shoot. Here's where Smart Presets really shine for me:

- **Batch Editing**: By using **Smart Presets**, I can apply consistent edits to a whole batch of photos without having to manually adjust each one. This is especially useful for events like weddings, where many images share similar lighting and composition.
- **Efficient Color Grading**: For portraiture or product photography, I create Smart Presets that auto-adjust **white balance** and **skin tones** based on the lighting conditions. I don't have to reapply these adjustments every time; Lightroom's AI takes care of it for me.
- **Auto Syncing**: With **Smart Presets**, I can automate syncing between devices, ensuring that the same adjustments are applied across my **desktop, mobile, and cloud devices**. This is ideal when I'm working from

multiple locations or need to access my edits on the go.

Tip: I use **metadata-based Smart Presets**, where Lightroom automatically applies certain edits based on keywords, ratings, or camera settings. For instance, I have a preset that applies a specific style to all photos shot with my **Canon EOS 5D Mark IV** camera.

Lightroom for Professional Photographers and Studios

For professional photographers and studio owners, Lightroom is an indispensable tool, offering powerful features that streamline **bulk editing**, **file management**, and **client deliveries**. As a designer, I rely heavily on Lightroom not just for editing, but also for managing my client's entire workflow—from shoot organization to final image delivery.

Key Features for Professional Photographers

1. **Advanced Metadata and Keyword Management**: One of the most valuable

tools for professional photographers is Lightroom's ability to handle extensive metadata. I can **tag** photos with detailed **keywords**, add **captions**, and even embed **GPS data** for easy organization and searchability. This is particularly helpful when managing large portfolios or when clients need to reference specific images quickly.

2. **Client-Specific Collections and Albums**: With Lightroom, I create **dedicated collections** for each client, keeping their images organized and easily accessible. I can also build **smart albums** that auto-collect photos based on certain criteria like **ratings**, **keywords**, or **file format**. This makes organizing images from multiple shoots incredibly efficient.

3. **Bulk Editing and Culling**: As a professional, I often need to cull through hundreds (or thousands) of images after a shoot. Lightroom's **Flagging**, **Rating**, and **Color Labeling** system helps me quickly sort through images, while **Auto Sync** and

Smart Presets ensure that edits are applied to large sets in seconds.

4. **Integrated Workflow with Photoshop**: For complex retouching or edits that require advanced features (like compositing or advanced color correction), Lightroom integrates seamlessly with **Photoshop**. I can easily round-trip images between Lightroom and Photoshop, preserving edits and metadata throughout the process.

5. **Streamlined Client Delivery**: With **Lightroom's Export Module**, I can quickly create deliverables for my clients, whether it's in **high-resolution** for print or **optimized files** for web and social media. Lightroom even allows me to export in a specific **file format** (such as TIFF, JPEG, or PNG) and to **apply watermarking** for branding.

Setting Up Lightroom for a Photography Studio

In a studio environment, multiple photographers or editors may work on a shared catalog of images.

Here's how I set up Lightroom to facilitate smooth studio operations:

- **Shared Catalogs**: By syncing catalogs via the **cloud**, all studio members can access the same images, no matter where they are. I make sure that all edits and metadata are synchronized across devices, ensuring consistency throughout the team.

- **Batch Export for Clients**: I often batch export multiple images with unique presets tailored for each client. Whether it's for a wedding, corporate shoot, or family portrait session, I can deliver a high-quality, customized selection of images all at once.

- **Cloud Backup and Storage**: By utilizing **Adobe's cloud storage**, I ensure that my studio's image files are backed up and securely stored. This is especially crucial in a professional setting, where client images need to be protected at all costs.

Optimizing Lightroom for Your Photography Business

Lightroom isn't just about editing—it's a complete **workflow solution** for photography businesses. Here's how I make sure Lightroom works for my studio:

- **Batch Import and Sorting**: During peak times, I need to get photos into Lightroom quickly. The **Import** function lets me bring in a batch of images, automatically applying my default **metadata, keywording**, and **presets** to each photo.
- **Client Folders**: Each project has a dedicated **folder and catalog**, and I use **collection sets** to keep everything organized. Whether it's an individual session or an event like a wedding, I know exactly where each file is located.
- **Collaborative Workflows**: Lightroom's ability to sync settings and edits across multiple devices means my team can work simultaneously on different tasks, whether it's editing, culling, or finalizing exports.

Tip: If you're managing a studio or handling high-volume work, it's critical to use **collections** and **smart collections** to keep things organized. Create collections based on different stages of your process—such as **Import**, **Culling**, **Editing**, and **Final Export**—so that you can track progress on any given project quickly.

For **professional photographers** and **studios**, Lightroom 2025 is more than just a photo editor; it's a powerful **workflow management tool**. By leveraging features like **Smart Presets**, **AI-powered automation**, and **cloud syncing**, I can automate my editing and keep my work organized, leaving more time for creativity. The flexibility and integration options available in Lightroom help me stay on top of my professional projects and maintain a high standard of work for my clients.

Chapter Ten

Tips, Troubleshooting, and Resources

In this final section, I'll share some **practical tips**, troubleshooting strategies, and essential **resources** that can enhance your experience with Lightroom 2025. As a seasoned **graphic designer** and **Lightroom user**, I've faced my fair share of challenges, but over the years, I've honed techniques to overcome them efficiently. Whether you're troubleshooting an issue or looking for ways to optimize your workflow, this section will offer useful solutions and guide you toward valuable learning materials.

Fixing Common Lightroom Issues

While Lightroom is a powerful tool, it's not immune to occasional hiccups. Understanding common issues and knowing how to fix them can save you time and frustration.

1. Lightroom Running Slowly

One of the most common issues I've encountered is slow performance, especially when dealing with large files or high-resolution images. Here's what I do to speed things up:

- **Optimize the Catalog**: Regularly optimize your catalog to keep it running smoothly. You can do this by going to **File > Optimize Catalog**. This cleans up unnecessary data and makes Lightroom more responsive.

- **Use Smart Previews**: If you're working with a large number of high-resolution images, use **Smart Previews** instead of the full-sized versions. These smaller files will reduce the load on your system, speeding up editing and navigation.

- **Turn Off GPU Acceleration**: While GPU acceleration can improve performance, it can also cause issues on certain machines. If Lightroom is sluggish, try disabling it by going to **Preferences > Performance** and unchecking **Use Graphics Processor**.

2. Missing or Corrupted Previews

Sometimes, Lightroom may fail to display the correct previews for your images, which can be frustrating.

- **Rebuild Previews**: To rebuild missing or corrupted previews, right-click on the affected folder in the Library module and select **"Build Smart Previews"** or **"Build All Previews"**.

- **Clear the Cache**: If previews are still not loading properly, clearing the **cache** might help. Go to **Edit** > **Preferences** > **Performance**, and click on **Purge Cache**.

3. Importing Problems

Another common issue is difficulty importing photos, especially when dealing with a large number of images or specific file formats.

- **Check File Permissions**: Ensure that Lightroom has the correct permissions to access your files. This is especially important if you're using **cloud storage** or external drives.

- **Update Lightroom**: Always keep Lightroom updated, as Adobe frequently releases patches to address import-related bugs.

Performance Optimization Tips

As a professional, efficiency and speed are essential when working with high volumes of photos. Here are some tips to ensure Lightroom performs at its best:

1. Upgrade Your Hardware

Lightroom is resource-intensive, especially when working with large files or performing complex edits. To ensure smooth performance, consider upgrading the following:

- **RAM**: Lightroom benefits from more memory, so if you're working with large image files or multiple catalogs, upgrading to **16 GB or more** of RAM can significantly boost performance.

- **SSD Storage**: Install Lightroom and your catalog on an **SSD** for faster read/write speeds. This will reduce lag when importing, exporting, and navigating through images.
- **Graphics Card**: A good **GPU** can speed up tasks like image rendering and applying edits, so ensure your system's graphics card is up to date.

2. Optimize Preferences for Speed

Lightroom gives you several ways to optimize the software's performance:

- **Use the Develop Module Only When Necessary**: When you're in the Library Module, try not to leave too many images loaded in the **Develop module** at once. It's more resource-intensive.
- **Limit Camera Raw Cache**: The **Camera Raw Cache** can quickly grow in size. Set it to a smaller size in **Preferences > Performance** (around 5-10 GB) to keep things efficient without using up too much disk space.

3. Manage Catalog Size

Large catalogs can slow down Lightroom. Here's how I manage them:

- **Use Multiple Catalogs**: For large projects or studio environments, split your catalog into smaller, manageable parts (e.g., one catalog for personal work and another for client work).
- **Regular Maintenance**: Regularly clean and optimize your catalog by going to **File > Optimize Catalog**.

Keyboard Shortcuts and Productivity Hacks

As an experienced Lightroom user, I rely heavily on keyboard shortcuts to boost my productivity. Here are some of my most-used shortcuts that help me stay efficient:

1. Essential Shortcuts

- **G** – Switch to **Grid View** (Library Module)
- **D** – Switch to **Develop Module**

- **E** – Switch to **Loupe View** (Library Module)
- **Ctrl/Cmd + Shift + E** – **Export** selected images
- **Ctrl/Cmd + Z** – Undo
- **Ctrl/Cmd + Shift + Z** – Redo
- **Q** – **Spot Removal Tool** (Develop Module)
- **T** – **Toggle Toolbar**
- **Ctrl/Cmd + Alt + N** – Create **New Collection**
- **R** – **Crop Tool** (Develop Module)

2. Time-Saving Editing Hacks

- **Auto Sync**: Use **Auto Sync** in the **Develop Module** to apply the same settings to multiple images at once. This saves time when editing similar shots, such as in a portrait or event shoot.
- **Copy & Paste Settings**: For quick adjustments, copy the settings from one photo by pressing **Ctrl/Cmd + Shift + C** and then paste them to another image using **Ctrl/Cmd + Shift + V**.

- **Solo Mode in Panels**: To focus on one editing tool at a time, enable **Solo Mode** by right-clicking on the panel headers in the **Develop Module**. This will collapse all other panels, allowing you to stay focused.

Recommended Plug-ins and Extensions

While Lightroom comes packed with tools, certain plug-ins and extensions can elevate your workflow. Here are some of my favorites:

1. Nik Collection by DxO

A collection of powerful editing tools that extend Lightroom's capabilities, particularly for **black-and-white** photography, **color correction**, and **sharpening**.

2. Luminar Neo

Luminar Neo adds advanced AI features for things like **sky replacement**, **portrait enhancement**, and **AI structure** adjustments, all integrated directly into Lightroom.

3. ON1 Resize AI

Perfect for those who need to resize images without losing detail, **ON1 Resize AI** leverages AI to increase image resolution for print purposes without introducing noticeable artifacts.

4. HDR Efex Pro

For photographers who work with HDR images, **HDR Efex Pro** provides powerful controls for blending multiple exposures into a seamless result.

Learning Resources, Communities, and Updates

As a **Lightroom user**, staying up-to-date with the latest features and engaging with the community is key to mastering the software.

1. Adobe's Official Tutorials

- Adobe offers **free tutorials** and **webinars** on their website and YouTube channel. Whether you're new to Lightroom or an experienced user, Adobe's resources are great for learning advanced techniques and discovering new tools.

2. Lightroom Communities

- **Reddit**: The **r/Lightroom** subreddit is a great place to ask questions, share tips, and find inspiration.
- **Lightroom Facebook Groups**: There are several active groups for both beginners and pros where users share editing workflows, presets, and troubleshooting tips.

3. Online Courses

- Websites like **Udemy**, **Skillshare**, and **LinkedIn Learning** offer in-depth Lightroom courses. I recommend **Glyn Dewis** and **Matt Kloskowski**, both of whom provide insightful and professional Lightroom training.

4. Stay Updated

- Regularly check for **Lightroom updates** to stay on top of new features and improvements. You can set Lightroom to **auto-update** in the **Creative Cloud app** to ensure you're always working with the latest version.

Lightroom is an incredibly powerful tool for photo editing, but like any software, it requires ongoing learning and adjustments to get the most out of it. By following these troubleshooting tips, optimizing your workflow, and utilizing keyboard shortcuts and smart plug-ins, you'll be able to work faster and more efficiently. Don't forget to explore the wealth of online resources available to deepen your knowledge and connect with the global Lightroom community.